PAIR-IT BOOKS®

This Is a School

Written by Martin Meyer

STECK-VAUGHN
ELEMENTARY · SECONDARY · ADULT · LIBRARY

A Harcourt Company

www.steck-vaughn.com

This is a school.

This is where children read.

This is where children sing.

This is where children play.

This is where children eat.

This is where children run.

This is where children learn!